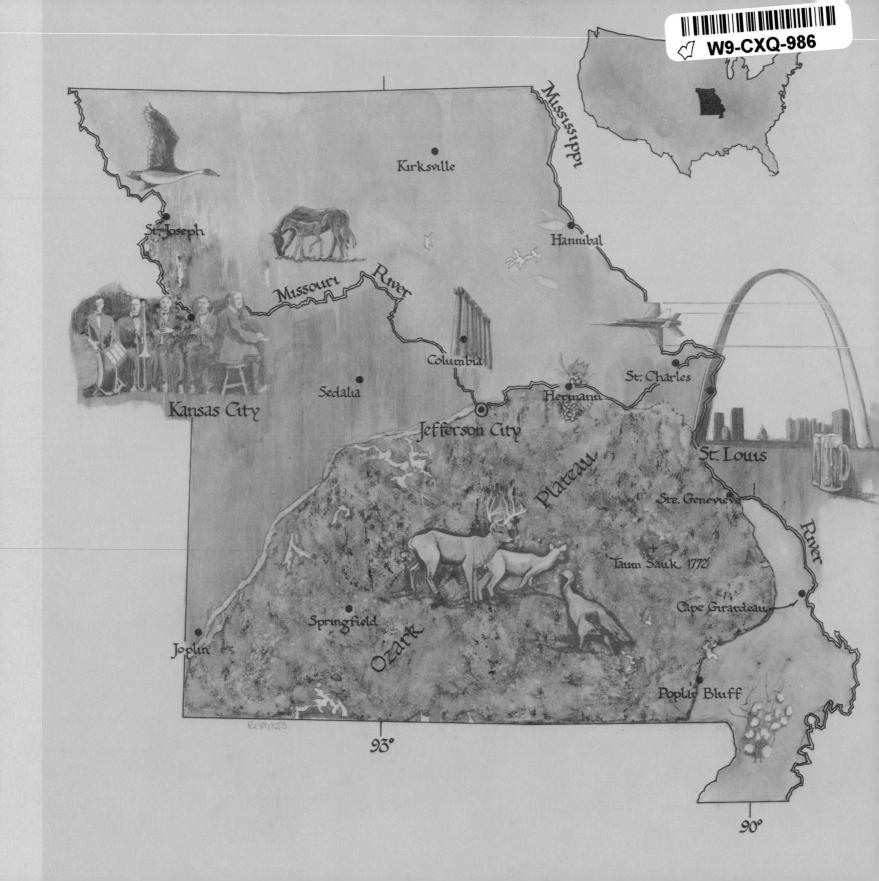

Kirksville

St. Joseph

Hannibal

Missouri   River

Columbia

Kansas City

Sedalia

St. Charles

Hermann

Jefferson City

St. Louis

Ste. Genevieve

Plateau

Taum Sauk 1772

Springfield

Ozark

Cape Girardeau

River

Joplin

Poplar Bluff

Mississippi

93°

90°

R. HAYNES

Foreword

From the Mississippi River to Kansas City, Missouri is a land rich in heritage and diverse in landscape.

It is a land of contrast where small towns exist harmoniously with thriving cities and where quiet farms dot a landscape that also contains bustling industry. Missouri is a state which remembers its history while looking ahead to a bright and promising future.

Centerre Bancorporation, like many others, is proud of Missouri. To express these sentiments, we are pleased to present *Missouri*. It is our particular pleasure to introduce *Missouri* at this time as we formally dedicate our new corporate headquarters building in St. Louis. What better way to commemorate this event than with a portrait of our state and its people.

New beginnings and milestones such as this one traditionally cause one to look back and reflect upon the past. *Missouri* is our way of showcasing our past and restating our commitment to its future.

We hope that you enjoy *Missouri* as much as we have enjoyed the examination of our state that culminates in the publication of this book. And we hope that you will agree with us that Missouri, in the heartland of America, deserves our best attention today, tomorrow, and beyond.

Chairman of the Board
and Chief Executive Officer
Centerre Bancorporation

MISSOURI
BY BILL NUNN

Mr. Peters

*At another day's end, his
face weathered by the suns
of many hayfields, he heads
for home near Taos.*

Central Missouri Farm
Osage County, east of Linn
U.S. Route 50

Missouri was a good enough country. A man could live, even if not fat, if he had a mind to work."

Lije Evans in *The Way West*
A. B. Guthrie, Jr.
Houghton Mifflin Company, 1949

Ozarks "knob" country
Stone County, southeast of Shell Knob
Route 86

*T*ain't no wonder 'tall, God rested
when He made these here hills.
He jest naturally had t'quit,
for He done his beatenest an'
war plumb gin out . . ."

"'Preacher Bill' who runs the ferry"
Harold Bell Wright
Shepherd of the Hills
Grosset, 1907

The Old Courthouse
St. Louis
Broadway at Market

*This city is a wonderful growth,
and if you would send out a
young man of energy to the
very best assurance of success,
send him here . . ."*

Ralph Waldo Emerson
Letter to brother, William
December 1852
Missouri Historical Review, October, 1963

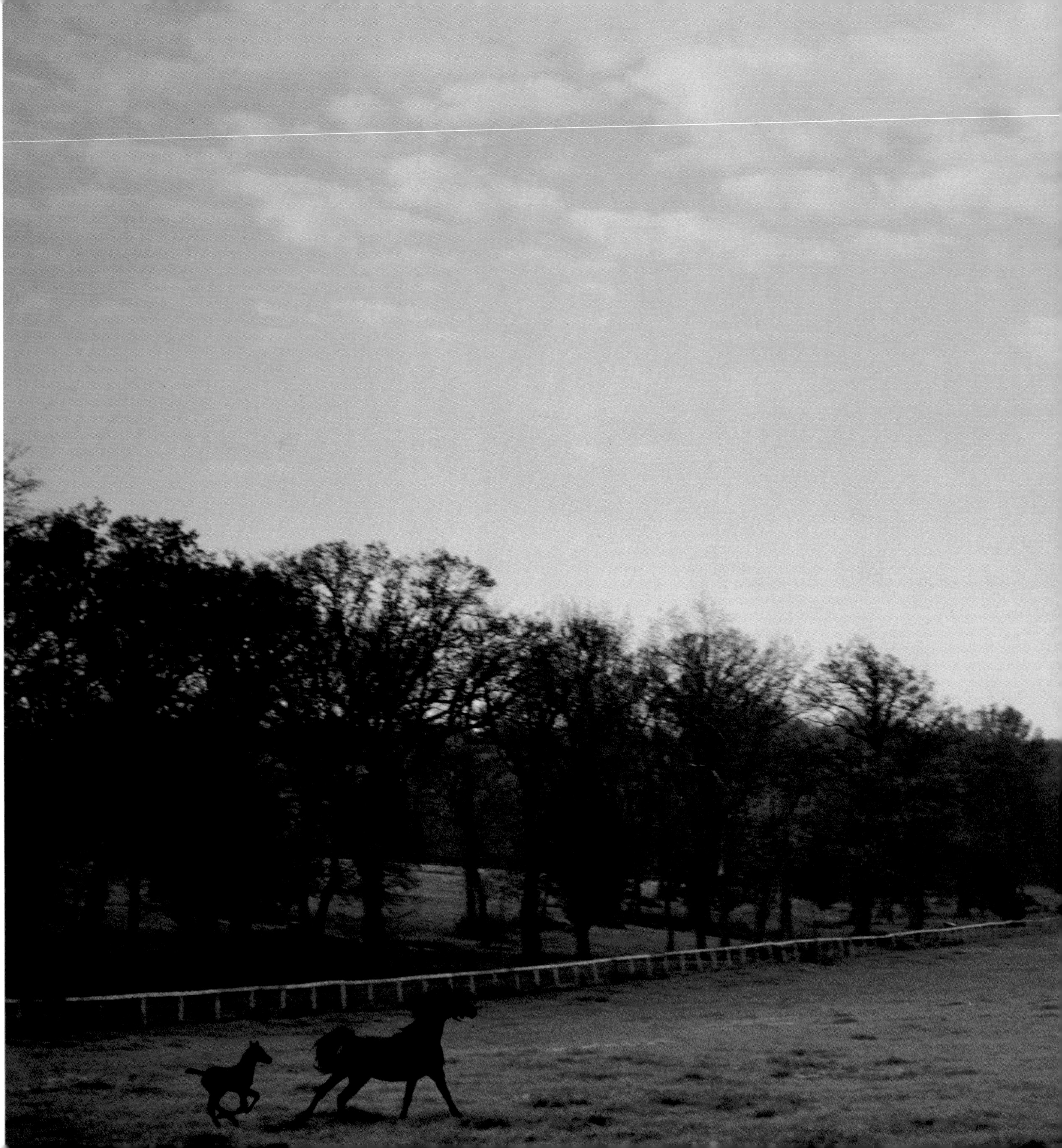

Saddle Horse Mare and Foal
Callaway Hills Farm
Callaway County

An old saying among horsemen
goes, 'If saddlers are "The Horse
America Made," they're also "The
Horse Missouri Made Better".'"

"Tales of a Little Dixie Horseman"
Joan Gilbert
Missouri Life
Volume 4, No. 2

Bridge over Lake Taneycomo
U.S. Route 65 at Branson
Taney County

M odern man is surrounded by
great achievements that don't work
very well—cities, the United Nations,
plumbing. Bridges work."

Andy Rooney
CBS Television Special Reports
"Bridges"

Hermann
On the Missouri River
Gasconade County

*T*hey envisioned a place where the
German heritage, culture and
language could be kept alive while, at
the same time, the advantages of
America could be enjoyed."

"Still a Morning Town"
Anna Hesse
Missouri Life
Volume 4, No. 1

Spanish Towers
Country Club Plaza
Kansas City

Who in Europe, or in America,
for that matter, knows that
Kansas City is one of the loveliest
cities on earth?"

Andre Maurois
I remember, I remember
Harper & Row, 1970

MISSOURI
BY BILL NUNN

Text and photographs
by Bill Nunn

Published by
Centerre Bancorporation
in cooperation with
The Lowell Press, Kansas City

Even in the fall, dogwood, Missouri's state tree, flashes its beauty with leaves daily changing colors—from reds to yellows to purplish browns and burgundies.

FROM TOP
Counterclockwise

Lambert Airport
St. Louis

Country Road
Newton County

Interstate 70
Warren County

Fall Color
Cole County

The "Katy"
Montgomery County

Winter Wheat
Callaway "Bottoms"

The Book Place
Platte City

"Leprechaun"
Little Dixie

"As it is the commendation of a good huntsman to find game in a wide wood, so it is no imputation if he hath not caught all."

Quoted by Walter Williams, Editor
The State of Missouri
The Missouri Commission to the
Louisiana Purchase Exposition, 1904

Missouri is . . .
Something Different

A<small>T THE</small> Mississippi River, I like to think, God said, "Now, I think I'll make something different, just for the hell of it."

So He put a little of all He'd made on His way West with the sun, then added a few extra pinches of special things.

Then He looked at what He'd made . . . and He laughed like the devil. And the place came to be called Missouri.

"Its geographical position has given the region dramatic importance in the history of national expansion, while its topography has tended to divide its people, its economy, and its political interests along sectional lines that have often resulted in confusion."

Missouri:
A Guide to the Show-Me State
Missouri State Highway Department, 1941

Morning Mist
Camden County

ACKNOWLEDGMENTS

A book like *Missouri* is the culmination of a special blend of talents. It is the result of many hours of deliberation and countless time in execution.

Missouri has emerged much like a fine piece of art. Bill Nunn, author and photographer of *Missouri,* examined the many attributes of the state and its place in history. Like an artist, each stroke, each picture taken and word put to paper was the result of painstaking effort to truly exemplify our grand state in a manner which befits its splendid heritage.

Providing the means with which to undertake this massive project was Centerre Bancorporation. The largest bank holding company in Missouri, Centerre is proud of St. Louis, Kansas City, Springfield and each of the markets it serves. This book provides Centerre with an opportunity to salute the state of Missouri and its people.

Finally, credit is also due to The Lowell Press, which has published this book in the quality fashion that befits this state where some five million people live and work and play—this place that is home to so many businesses and individuals.

Library of Congress Cataloging in Publication Data

Nunn, Bill.
Missouri

1. Missouri—Description and travel—1981-
2. Missouri—Social life and customs. I. Title.
F470.N86   977.8   82-15376
ISBN 0-91504-77-7   AACR2
ISBN 0-913504-78-5 (pbk.)

The paper in this book meets the guidelines for permanence and durability of the Committee on Production Guidelines for Book Longevity of the Council on Library Resources.

FIRST EDITION
Copyright © 1982 by W. R. Nunn

Printed in the United States of America
by The Lowell Press, Inc., Kansas City, Missouri

This book is dedicated
to Ma,
who was always ready to go,
and to Pa,
who usually took her

"My daddy always told me, 'You've got to find
something where you lost it. . . .'"

Ralph Gideon
"The Ozarks: 'I been on this place 84 years'"
Clay Anderson, *American Mountain People*
National Geographic Society, 1978

Contents

". . . The state is a literal checkerboard, the crossroads of almost everything."

John Gunther
Inside U.S.A.
Harper & Brothers, 1947

From Four Corners, a Center

At Jefferson City, the capital, in the center of Missouri, the U.S. Routes 54-63 bridge connects north with south, spanning the Missouri River flowing from its birth in the high country of the West to the East and its meeting with the Mississippi ten miles north of St. Louis.

To get from here to there over its many streams and deep valleys, Missouri has some six thousand bridges on its state highway system alone enough to span 250 miles.

WE MISSOURIANS, at least a tad more than most people, rather savor the notion that we and this stretched-out, side-bulging rectangle where we live are . . . well, "different." And the notion is far from far-fetched.

Out West, during this nation's putting-together, the engineers and the surveyors, following the dictates of the politicians, staked out a unique geo-political oddity known as Four Corners. There, in the arid reaches of the Southwest, corners of Utah, Colorado, Arizona and New Mexico meet in plumb-line preciseness to make an imaginary dot on the map of the United States. And even a dainty-slippered woman could stand in four states, all at the same time, should she so desire, whilst the tumbleweeds skitter across her feet.

But this man-drawn oddity is a piker (derivation: Pike County, Missouri) compared to Nature's own creation in this place the mapmakers pencilled in as The State of Missouri.

Smack-dab in the center of the country (Well, almost. In Missouri, "close" counts in dancing and horseshoe pitching and locating places . . . as in "Over yonder," or "Down the road there a piece."), Missouri forms a 69,000-square-mile, 45-million-acre "corner" where North and South, East and West lap over each other.

And this lap-over land is fertile ground for the state's clichéd—but honest truly—diversity.

From it blooms an array of mind-boggling aggregations of flora and fauna, wide-swinging climatological pendulums, bubbling pots of un-melted ethnic groups, a kaleidoscope of colorful history and checkered politics, age-old traditions and quaint customs, innovators and stand-patters, shakers and movers, and watchers and doers.

It's a place that defies succinct description. Or even a lengthy one. And that very "Show Me" defiance challenges native son and stranger alike to try it.

It's also a place that makes that attempt—albeit knowingly futile—satisfying and interesting, downright fascinating.

In thirty years a man can see a lot, if he looks. And he can hear a lot, if he listens. And with a modicum of attention, he should come to know a place . . . at least a little.

But just when I think I've come to know this Missouri fairly well, it changes. Or I see some of it I never saw before. Or in a way I never thought of before.

But at its center, some things about Missouri never change—its solid sameness, leavened with sprinkles of "What's next?"; its comfortableness, with occasional awe; its beauty, with sufficient commonness to make it recognizable . . . and appreciated; its "wears well" durableness, for a while . . . or for a lifetime.

That's the Missouri I hope you'll find here.

26

" 'Tis the greatest crossroads the world has ever seen."

Senator Thomas Hart Benton

Where It All Began

"Just above this stream (River Des Peres) the bluff rose high again. Then it leveled off. The river arched eastward. Back from this arc, terraces rose gradually . . .

"Laclede notched a few trees, then sped downstream to Fort Chartres. When we landed, Laclede walked up to Commandant Noyen de Villiers. No one could forget the look in his eyes as he said, 'I have found the place. Someday it will be one of the finest cities on the whole continent.'"

William Barnaby Faherty
Wide River Wide Land
Piraeus Publishers, 1976

PRECEDING PAGE

Thirty years after Luther Ely Smith, Sr., envisioned the concept, the first triangular stainless-steel section of the Gateway Arch was installed in February of 1963 on its foundation for which the first concrete was poured June 27, 1962.

After World War II had halted the project, civic leaders in 1946 raised $225,000 by subscription for prize money in an architectural design competition. Out of 172 entries, five were awarded $10,000 each in 1948. First prize of $50,000 was awarded to Eero Saarinen for the 630-foot arch, an underground Museum of Westward Expansion and a landscaped park.

The Arch

"From its pioneering role in the settlement of the West to the part it plays today as a major center for the development of those tools used in outer space exploration, Missouri has frequently been in the forefront of the significant drama of national growth with leadership and resources to meet the needs of the times."

William Parrish
A History of Missouri
University of Missouri Press, 1971

THE GATEWAY ARCH.

It graces the banks of the mighty river coursing ceaselessly below it . . . the Mississippi, geographically cleaving half a continent and industriously uniting a free Republic.

Its shimmering stainless steel sheath reflects—with the whims of weather—the changing play of sun and cloud, of moon and star. Resiliently it withstands the snows of winter, the rains of springtime, the suns of summer and the winds of all seasons in Missouri.

In monumental simplicity, it tells the world, "This is St. Louis."

And symbolically, bedrock-solid in historic ground and sky-reaching in its vision of tomorrow, it proclaims, "This is where it all began." Not just a state, but the fullness of an entire nation.

That's the way events often happened in Missouri. And they still do.

The Old Courthouse was the site of the Dred Scott case, a factor in bringing slavery to a crisis—and the Civil War.

The City

"For me, the spirit of St. Louis is a unique blend of all that is best in America."

John Hanley
Chairman of the Board, Monsanto Company
St. Louis COMMERCE
April, 1981

IN THE shadow of the great Arch, across two centuries they carry—the sights and the smells, the sounds and the voices of a restless, energetic people building a frontier fur trading post into one of the world's great cities . . .

The scrunch and squeak of Laclede's bateau, pushing ashore in Mississippi mud amid December cold of 1763 . . . and the whack of axe against tree in February of '64 as his thirty men, led by fourteen-year-old Auguste Chouteau, cleared the ground for a new town here on the high, western bank of the river in a long sweeping curve about ten miles below its confluence with the muddy Missouri . . .

The volley of cannon March 9, 1804, as the Spaniard, Delassus, and the American, Amos Stoddard, exchanged flags at the Government House as Captain Meriwether Lewis witnessed the formal termination of Spanish authority in Upper Louisiana . . .

The lavish celebrations, following months of planning and organizing by Lewis and Captain William Clark, leading to the shoving-off from Wood River of the Expedition to the Pacific in May of 1804 . . .

The noisy hoopla when the primitive *Zebulon M. Pike* docked on August 2, 1819, signalling the colorful era of the ever-bigger and ostentatious steamboats, sparking decades of spectacular growth as St. Louis emerged as one of the nation's leading cities . . .

The lilting *chansonnettes* of Ashley's band of one hundred that spring of 1822 when, as John Neihardt lyricized in his epic *Cycle of the West,*

In Kiener Plaza, with the Old Courthouse and the Gateway Arch behind him, the statue of The Olympic Runner adds its own symbolism to the "new" St. Louis.

In his unique wound-spring stance, Stan "The Man" Musial stands at the entrance to Busch Memorial Stadium, home of the St. Louis baseball and football Cardinals.

Anheuser-Busch bought the baseball Cardinals in 1953. The stadium, a key in the redevelopment of downtown St. Louis, was dedicated in May, 1966.

With its circular shape and cantilevered canopy, fans can see, unobstructed, anywhere on the field from any seat in the 50,000-seat stadium.

Afternoon sun outlines the Anheuser-Busch Barley House on St. Louis's South Side.

The world's largest producer of beer, Anheuser-Busch, Inc., has led the U.S. brewing industry for a quarter of a century. Its beer sales in 1981 set an all-time industry record with 54.5 million barrels—29 percent of the national market.

Budweiser outsells all other brands in the world—and more than one of every four beers sold in the United States is a product of Anheuser-Busch, Inc.

"St. Louis is fortunate to be big enough to afford topflight cultural and athletic events and yet small enough to remain a family-oriented community."

Armand Stalnaker, Former Chairman
General American Life Insurance Company
St. Louis COMMERCE
April, 1981

"tales of wealth, out-legending Peru, came wind-blown from Missouri's distant springs . . . ."

The dead-serious carousings of the fur trappers, back home in civilization, drinking and women-ing and good-timing before heading West again on the trail of the thick-pelted beaver . . .

The guttural speech of emigrant Germans adding to the city's language—already heavily laced with cultured English, musical French, lively Spanish, and earthy "American Frontier"—as some thirty to forty thousand Germans settled here between 1840 and 1850 to escape religious and political persecution in their homeland . . .

The hammering of spikes as the Pacific Railroad, later the Missouri Pacific, started in 1850 as the first railroad in Missouri . . . to be joined by five others with terminals in the city by the time the first shot was fired in the Civil War . . .

The ten-thousand-dollar fireworks at the gala Fourth of July, 1874, opening of Eads ("The Impossible") Bridge, which scuttled the steamboats by carrying the goods of a booming nation on east-west trains across the Mississippi . . . and the degeneration of the once-bustling waterfront into a ramshackle warehouse and dwelling area . . .

The hurdy-gurdy of the summer-long World's Fair of 1904, when twenty million people filed through the gates out west in Forest Park . . . and the whole nation would learn to sing "Meet me in St. Louis, Louie . . ."

The whirring of machinery making things as St. Louis and the

"This latter block (staked out by Laclede) contains the only tract in the original townsite which has never changed hands. The Basilica of St. Louis, the King—the Old Cathedral—still stands on this hallowed ground."

Gregory Franzwa
The Old Cathedral
The Patrice Press, 1980

nation prospered from the industrial needs of World War I and the boom years of the Twenties . . .

The toe-tapping rhythms of the brassy jazz, imported upriver from New Orleans, blaring loud and syncopated "down on the levee" from the riverboat bands like Fate Marable's with downriver musicians like Louie Armstrong . . .

The 1933 vision of Luther Ely Smith, Sr., of clearing the blighted old waterfront to create a national monument to the Louisiana Purchase and the nation's westward expansion . . .

And trucks still rumbling on its cobblestone streets . . .

Then the sounds of jackhammers and steel-driving men and the grinding of big machinery as men strove to make, with concrete and steel, the visionary catenary curve of Eero Saarinen that would be The Arch . . .

And, from up on the hill at Cafe Louie's at Third and Delmar, the enthusiastic crusading of Jimmy Massucci to save Laclede's Landing . . . followed by the practical plans and thoughtful reasoning and leadership of men like Bill Maritz . . .

Until, once again, in the Seventies, came the laughter and the clinking of glass, the smell of good food, the clomp of footsteps on the old cobblestones, the doing of business in the refurbished old stores and warehouses . . .

The hum of business and the living of the good life, back here in the shadow of the Arch, at Laclede's Landing . . .

Where it all began.

The Old Cathedral is the oldest west of the Mississippi, begun in 1831. The first major example of Greek Revival architecture in Missouri, it once was the Mother Church for Roman Catholics in more than half of the United States.

The newest "jewel" in St. Louis's renaissance, Centerre Plaza centers around the state's largest office building.

The 31-story building and bank complex was built by Centerre, IBM and The Equitable Life Assurance Society.

Rising majestically behind it is the classic Civil Courts Building.

Missouri is . . .
Its People

Clarence C. Barksdale

IN LAW SCHOOL he decided, "Bankers, as I analyzed it, were becoming community leaders, not lawyers."

So, Clarence C. Barksdale, whose grandfather was Governor of Missouri from 1928-32, left Washington University Law School. Instead, he began a career that would earn for him the title of chairman of the state's largest banking company and recognition as one of the key civic leaders in Missouri.

If his analyses were correct, Cedge Barksdale would first need to establish himself in the St. Louis banking community—his home. He entered First National Bank in St. Louis' executive training program in 1958 and quickly advanced through management positions.

In 1970, at the age of 37, he was appointed president of the bank, the youngest person to become president of a major St. Louis bank. Six years later in 1976, he was chairman and chief executive officer of the bank. In 1977, he was one of a few men highlighted in an article in the *New York Times:* "Youth Takes Over in Corporate St. Louis." A year later, he was named chairman and chief executive officer of First Union Bancorporation, now Centerre Bancorporation.

While all of this was going on, Cedge remembered what influenced his decision to go into banking: the desire to be a community leader.

Missouri has many banks—a handful of large ones. But the state has few men—bankers or others—who rival Clarence Barksdale when it comes to concern for this state. He's never flinched from taking on the tough issues when the future of St. Louis, Kansas City, or Missouri was at stake. In the forefront or behind the scenes, he's never turned down working for a cause he believes in. Whether it's helping to lay the groundwork for a Coro program in Missouri or dedicating a neighborhood redevelopment office in the City of St. Louis, Barksdale is involved.

He'd rather be a doer than a talker—leading fund-raising efforts for United Way, raising marketing funds for the Port of Metropolitan St. Louis, serving on the boards (at one time or another) of every major organization in St. Louis, and serving his community as president of Civic Progress, Inc., an organization composed of the CEOs of major corporations headquartered in St. Louis.

Quality of life is a recurring theme of Clarence C. Barksdale. "It's a key issue—it's something we in Missouri have, and it's something we have to protect. Quality of life, it's so hard to achieve and so easy to lose."

Barksdale says that he serves his state and his St. Louis home in order to protect its quality of life. "If you strive to be a leader and then attain it, you have to accept the accompanying responsibilities," he says. "I chose this course a number of years ago. It's always a balancing act between family and work and civic responsibilities. Fortunately, my wife, Nini, and I share the same opinion—you must earn the right to be proud of your city, of your state. That means working on behalf of both of them."

For Clarence C. Barksdale, it means combining corporate excellence with civic responsibilities—a task he continues to manage in Missouri.

"The real challenge is to take what you've got and make it grow. That's how you motivate people."

Clarence Barksdale
St. Louis Business Journal
December 22-28, 1980

Barksdale has led community fund-raising drives, has been a member or director of every major organization in St. Louis—and has led most of them. He has received national citations in publications like Time *and the* New York Times.

"There's a lot of Missouri in Missouri still"

A LOT OF people have tried to explain Missouri. And Lord knows it can stand plenty.

But doing it is akin to trying to trace the ancestry of one of its celebrated mules: you can only go so far.

Like the mule, Missouri is a hybrid, born of recognized parents, but a hell-raising one-of-a-kind, a breed all its own.

It's a proud one. And intelligent, too, with a mind of its own. It's hard to budge, but once it gets goin' it'll work like hell. It's got a gleam in its eye and a "mean streak" in its character, some folks say. Just ornery, others call it.

Such an offspring is best talked about in romantic, even mystical, terms—ambiguous phrases or poetry, maybe. The trick is to make a little say a lot. It can't all be said anyway—all of the historical facts that shame fiction, all the legends that enhance the facts, all the tall tales with grains of truth, all the truths that strain credulity . . .

George Wallace did it best. The state was his "beat" for the Kansas City *Star*, and for the edification of the paper's epigramming funnyman, Bill Vaughan, he explained it all in one sentence:

"There's a lot of Missouri in Missouri still."

Later, Vaughan said, "I asked him what in the world he meant, and he said he hadn't the slightest idea. But he knew what he meant and so did I, and so do any of you who are Missourians, even though it would be hard to put it into words."

But legion are they who have tried.

Walter Williams, founder of the world's

"I have lived all my life in this state, but if someone were to ask me if I knew Missouri, I would have to ask, 'Which Missouri do you mean?'"

"Bill Vaughan's Missouri"
Missouri Historical Review
Volume LVIII, No. 2

One of the nation's largest, Missouri's state highway system covers 32,000 miles . . . from trans-continental, traffic-moving Interstates like 70 and 44 to Route HH, a daisy-lined supplementary road in Newton County.

And with the need to get from here to there over its many streams and valleys, Missouri needs bridges—like this underslung arched bridge over the Current River on Route 19 in Shannon County, one of six thousand on the state system.

first school of Journalism at the University of Missouri and a dedicated stickler for truth and fact, declared flatly:

"The plain unvarnished truth about Missouri is superlative."

John Gunther was earthier. After looking over the whole *Inside U.S.A.*, he concluded, "Missouri has the reflexes of its own celebrated mules. It's a state with a kick in it."

William Parrish took an historian's long view:

"During the years since its tumultuous entry into the Union of States, Missouri has played a major role in both regional and national development."

MacKinlay Kantor, the Iowa-born Pulitzer prize-winning author, romanticized the state unabashedly:

"I fell in love with Missouri before I ever walked her soil . . . much as a young man may have a Dream Dolores whom he's never touched, an Imagined Ingrid whose perfume he's never scented . . . yet he feels his pulse beginning to pound when her name is mentioned."

Knowing her better—or at least longer—he later decided:

"Missouri is . . . spooky."

IT ALL depends on how you look at this place, and from where and when. But there's a lot of it to look at . . . and wonder about.

Alaska is roughly eight times bigger than Missouri. But that's counting snow and ice, too.

Texas could brag about being four times the size of Missouri. But even Texas, surely, wouldn't do that, seeing as how the Lone Star State was conceived here and midwifed by the son of its father. And Texas has so honored Stephen Austin of little Potosi, Missouri, by naming its capital for him.

Among the fifty states, Missouri comes in nineteenth for size and fifteenth for population. But such categories dodge any ranking for diversity.

California, perhaps, might outdo Missouri in variety—with its "real" mountains, fruitful valleys and arid deserts, and a sea coast running the entire length down its bent elbow. But if a Missourian wanted to haggle about it—and some would—he could point out that the landlocked Lake of the Ozarks has more miles of shoreline than the Golden State.

Besides, what Missouri doesn't have within its own borders, it "borrows" from its neighbors. (There are eight of them, more than any other state except Tennessee.) And that's fair enough, because Missouri gave most of them "a starter" for their crop of distinction.

Illinois, granted, was there first, on the east. So, above the Missouri River where the glacial, black-rich soil stopped, Missouri borrows some of it. Going west from the Mississippi, it takes just enough of this land to balance that hardscrabble, rocky ground down south—and it lets Iowa keep the most of it, to justly earn its reputation for corn and hogs.

From its northeast corner, at Athens and Alexandria, where it borrows (or intended to) memories of the glories of ancient Greece and Egypt, Missouri hugs the Mississippi for some five hundred winding miles south—past Hannibal and Louisiana and St. Louis and "The Cape" to the alluvial lowlands of the Bootheel delta country where it kisses Kentucky and Tennessee.

They were states, too, when Missouri—at long last—was admitted into the Union in

"The Missourians . . . feel that true independence flows from a conviction that their own physical exertions are equal to every call, necessity and emergency of life."

Henry Rowe Schoolcraft

The Grimes Golden, a Stark Bro's apple, is one variety that is self-pollinating . . . although this moth may think he's helping.

Not as extensive as they once were in Missouri, apple orchards still dot the countryside around Marionville (above) in Lawrence County, Weston in Platte County and Waverly on the Missouri River in Lafayette County.

1821. And they sent a lot of people here, people like Daniel Boone, looking for new land and more space and new beginnings. And they reach out fingertips to touch the upstart they helped populate.

A fellow named John Hardeman Walker gave Arkansas a perpetual kick-in-the-head when he persuaded the Drawers-of-State-Lines to give Missouri the Bootheel, a stripling of the Old South lying between the Mississippi and the St. Francis rivers. But after that heel-gouging of its southern neighbor, Missouri heads due west, friendly sharing the forested, hilly Ozarks with Arkansas along the way—even leaving her some of the highest mountains and prettiest streams.

Over west, they both share some of the red-dirt edges of Oklahoma territory—just enough for the feel of it, blowing in the face on winds from the Great Southwest.

Then it's northbound, straight as an arrow, up the side of Kansas, until it splits the metropolis sitting astride the line. From there it's slower going, following the wanderings of the brawling Missouri River on up to Nebraska.

Along the way it gave Nebraska and Kansas all of that land beyond the mouth of the Kaw and back along the Osage and the Platte, the Great Plains country rolling relentlessly, imperceptibly upward to the eastern face of the Rocky Mountains.

And it gave a whole nation a way west . . . and the people to lead it.

Some say "Mizzour-ee." Some say "Mizzour-ah." Or "Mizzour-a." And they're all from—and talking about—the same place.

But that's only the name of this place—not the real meat of everyday talk, the important

"... Every farmer grows grapes sufficient for home wine, and Hermann, county seat (Gasconade County), is the location of Stone Hill wine cellars, largest east of California."

The State of Missouri
Missouri Commission to the
Louisiana Purchase Exposition, 1904

In the early 1900s, when Missouri ranked second in U.S. wine production, Stone Hill Winery was the third largest in the world and the second in the nation.

During Prohibition its cellars grew mushrooms, but in 1969 the James Helds leased it and again began operating it as a winery, making it one of the leaders in the restoration of Missouri as a wine-producing state. Recently, the region near Augusta was named the nation's first officially recognized winemaking district.

things of life in this place . . .

In the downtown cafes of Faucett and Platte City and Weston, and in the new restaurant out on the interstate, they eat oven-warm peach or apple pie for a mid-morning snack. And they talk about tobacco.

"Too wet this year," the young man said, explaining about "spikes" and how fast a good hand could strip two rows of the "brown gold" in no time at all. "A lot of it's smelly, like that batch on the wagon by the warehouse."

On up north—past "St. Joe" to Rock Port and Phelps City, around Fairfax and Skidmore and over east to Hamilton and Chillicothe—they wear cowboy hats and John Deere bill caps, and they smoke cigarettes and chomp on cigars over a cleaned-up plate of bacon (or steak) and eggs, and they talk about cattle. And the accent smacks of the Great Plains, the big cattle country just across the Missouri.

They talk of corn, too, and hogs—and of tests and term papers and tenure—at Tarkio and Maryville, academic centers in this crop-growing land.

Around Trenton they wonder about the popcorn crop, and down around Brunswick and Salisbury they josh passers-through about it raining pecans when they shake the trees in the groves of the Grand River bottoms. And at Unionville they talk about the annual sale in "The Feeder Calf Capital of the World."

In the Monterrey Restaurant on the outskirts of Mexico, the city "Doc" in full hunting attire and his country friend in work clothes swap stories of quail flushed and dogs cussed . . . and the days left in the season.

"Ever' mornin' when I wake up achin' and groanin', I swear I'll never go again," Jess grins. "Then 'bout noon I start feelin' pretty good

. . . and the next thing you know I've got those dogs loaded up and we're off again." And "Doc" wishes he could go with him.

At lunchtime in the Main Street cafes of Edina and Shelbina, in Paris and Palmyra, they eat the Plate Lunch Special and ponder the imponderables of the weather and what it'll do to the soybeans and the corn and the milo.

"It's been 'way too wet . . . but it's time to be gettin' 'em in, mud or not, if I can get in the field."

Some three hundred miles away, down in the Bootheel, at the bank or the gin, they talk about King Cotton—or maybe more soybeans—in the soft drawl where the r's become h's and where the South starts to take its own good time all the way to New Orl'ns.

In the center of the state, carpooling from Jefferson City back home to Linn and Westphalia and Eldon and California, across the river to Holts Summit and New Bloomfield, they hash over the everyday business of state government, of legislative shenanigans, of lobbyists and politics.

Southwest, around Springfield, dusk settles over the Ozarks highlands and tiptoes along the ridges and seeps into the valleys. And they swig the last swallow of coffee (". . . with plenty of that good stuff with all that butterfat"), or down the last beer before heading home in the pickup. It's milking time in Grade A dairy land.

More and more, it's beef country, too, on land where the grazing's good. Or where they can make it so, seeding once-gullied hillsides where corn or tomatoes or strawberries couldn't hold the thin soil.

And in this old land with old ways they're adapting to newcomers—like Texans accustomed to running big spreads, and Limousins

". . . Bagnell Dam, the last big privately-funded dam in America, had dramatically reshaped the face of mid-America—as, later, it was to re-shape the vacation and retirement plans of millions of mid-Americans."

"Lake of the Ozarks"
Missouri Life Volume 3, No. 1

Once a region of small, home-owned resorts and cabins, the lake area has become a major convention and vacation center, with posh resorts like Tan-Tar-A and Lodge of the Four Seasons leading the way, luring pleasure-seekers from all over the Midwest with yachting, speedboating, skiing, fishing . . .

and Charolais, new breeds they're running on them.

In modern corporation offices, lights burn brightly in St. Louis's early evening gray. The secretaries are gone (after "Would you make that reservation for me in the morning to New York?" . . . or London or Singapore or Los Angeles), and shirt-sleeved executives wind up the day's last meeting. Slipping back into suit coats, they head for yet another board meeting, or a quiet drink before dinner at a swank restaurant. Or an evening "out" in Powell Hall listening to the symphony or watching a live performance of a Broadway show at the American Theatre. Then home, late, in Ladue or Clayton.

Two hundred and fifty miles to the west, via Interstate 70, or thirty minutes by jet, Kansas Citians stream from offices and banks and stores rising from the roller-coaster hills of skyscraping downtown, or from Crown Center or the Country Club Plaza or from outlying suburban industrial parks.

They talk of going "back home this week-

And in the winter it's a quiet place . . . where the wind tugs at the mainsail, and the lines slap against the mast, and a sailor's alone with the sounds of boat and water . . . and his own private sunset.

"I never saw such corn in my life . . . . When we come to gathering it, we will have to take ladders to climb up to the ears."

Robinson Garnett Smith, in letter to Kentucky relatives
"Bounty of the Fields"
Official Manual of the State of Missouri, 1979-80

Mr. Smith may have stretched the truth . . . by a few years. But corn does grow tall, after luxuriant tasseling, in the Missouri bottoms near Wooldridge in Cooper County. And the smell of new-mown hay fills the late evening air along the Moreau River in Cole County, and a lone car swims through a sea of ripened wheat on Route 50 in Johnson County. Late evening sun bathes an Osage River farm in a golden glow twelve miles east of Jefferson City.

end"—to Iowa or Oklahoma or Nebraska, Missouri or Kansas. Or for a week of skiing at Aspen, or on a vacation this summer at Lake of the Ozarks.

And here where Robert Van Horn declared to cheers that "The West is found!" many drive home in cars with Kansas license plates—to mansions in Mission Hills and Prairie Village, to Overland Park and Leawood, or to one of the half-dozen subdivisions constantly sprouting from the Kansas prairie . . .

And they are Missourians all.

AFTER He'd put it all together, then standing back and watching the goings-on in this place, there must've been times when He wondered if maybe He had overdone things.

At times it seemed as if a whole lot of "gee-in'" and "haw-in'" went on here. The people kicked up an ungodly racket every now and then. More than most, it seemed.

They were . . . well, different. But He guessed He'd sort of molded them that way, what with the kind of place He'd put them in. They'd sure added to what He'd given them to work with . . . all in a short time, too, by His watch.

Why, just look at it . . .

It's tough as a boot, ornery and bull-headed. And it's Southern-lady genteel.

It's filthy rich and hardscrabble poor.

It's pretty as a picture and homely as a mongrel dog.

It's as old as sin, made in Eden, and it's as new as space capsules, homemade at McDonnell-Douglas in St. Louis.

It's as changeable as next hour's weather and as bedrock-steady as the impermeable rhyolite porphyry of the Johnson Shut-Ins.

It's as busy as a traffic patrolman in Columbia after a University football game on a Saturday afternoon in October . . . and it's slow-moving as a lizard sunning on an Ozark dolomite glade.

It's Lindbergh Boulevard and Southwest Trafficway clogged with five-o'clock drivers . . . and it's a dusty country road leading back to yesterday.

It's where "Everything is up to date in Kansas City," as lyricized and set to music by Rodgers and Hammerstein. And it's where colorful, earthy remnants of near-Chaucerian speech hangs on in the Ozarks hills, searched out and recorded by Vance Randolph.

It's hundreds of people camped in trailers and RV's in the woods around Dixon, playing and listening for days to authentic bluegrass guitar-pickin' and fiddlin'. And it's two hundred thousand people crammed onto the Mississippi riverfront to hear Ella Fitzgerald sing as high as the Gateway Arch and as low-

"At the age of eleven (in 1887), Dad shipped one crate of peony cut flowers to Omaha in a carload of strawberries. The wholesaler sent him three dollars . . . Dad continued to grow peonies the rest of his life."

Allen Wild on the start of Gilbert H. Wild & Son, Inc.
Jo Ellis, "The Peripatetic Peony"
Missouri Life, Volume 5, No. 1

"Flowers from the Wilds of Missouri" come from more than two hundred acres near Sarcoxie in Jasper County, the largest peony and day lily fields in the world.

And Fall's gourds, squash and pumpkins, from many of the area's farmers, come to "town" in a pickup truck for sale on the square at Neosho, the county seat of Newton County.

down as an old-time Bootheel cotton picker's blues.

It's plush, "together" living in highrise Mansion House apartments on the St. Louis waterfront . . . and it's as unpeopled and solitary as the "Who, who, who are you?" of a hoot owl riding the night breeze in the Irish Wilderness.

It's the newest chemical discovery from Monsanto, and it's the aged-in-the-barrel sippin' whiskey from McCormick's Distillery.

It's where millions flock yearly to see Old Matt's Cabin in the Shepherd of the Hills country, and where thousands work daily in St. Louis's brawny glass-and-steel Mercantile Towers and the soft bronze-tinted Centerre Plaza—and work and live in "total community" Crown Center, Hallmark-built in Kansas City "for those who want the very best."

It's the one-and-only American Royal, spread over acres in Kansas City. And it's Louis Sullivan's Wainwright Building, the first to scrape the sky in St. Louis, or anywhere else.

It's where gentle Eugene Field's "Gingham Dog and the Calico Cat, side by side on the table sat . . ."—and where Mallinckrodt Chemical Works produced the first pure uranium for Enrico Fermi's experimental atomic bomb.

It's as modern as nuclear energy to come from Union Electric's Callaway plant, and it's as outmoded as an outdoor john in the Ozarks backwoods.

It's as hectic as a stand-up lunch at Woolworth's and as unhurried as a cane pole fisherman on a Swampeast slough.

It's music is as country as Porter Waggoner,

the West Plains Flash, and as twangy as the Kendalls, Roy and Jeannie, of Bridgeton. It's as ragtimey as Scott Joplin, that "diminished fifth man" from Sedalia and St. Louis, and as bouncy as "Twelfth Street Rag" from Kansas City. It's as bluesy as W.C. Handy, as jazzy as Clark Terry and his searing trumpet, and it's as classical as young Leonard Slatkin with the temerity to tour the East with his St. Louis Symphony Orchestra and come back with rave reviews.

It's George Washington Carver, born in slavery at Diamond Grove, and it's Margaret Bush of St. Louis, the first woman president of the NAACP.

It's Champ Clark of Bowling Green who, by all odds, should've been President, and wasn't. And it's Harry S Truman who, by all odds, shouldn't have been . . . but sure as hell was.

Missouri is timeless rivers, called mighty. And it's ancient hills, called mountains.

It's "dust-kickin'" history, one of a kind. And it's today, making more of the same . . . with its own stamp on tomorrow.

It's cities, big ones, full of the know-how of business and the making of things. And it's small towns and farms, full of open spaces and the growing of things. And it's people knowing how to live, wherever they are.

It's a place where a lot of things started and some ended . . . and where some things it started will never end . . .

Because there's a lot of Missouri in Missouri still . . . and in almost everywhere.

After running the gamut of its distinctive blossoming, the dogwood still graces the woodlands with its "plain" green leaves of summer, upper right.

Missouri is . . .
The Dogwood

"Legend has is that dogwood once grew straight and tall like other trees. It was chosen to be used as the cross which bore Christ. Jesus, in His mercy for the tree, promised that never again would it grow tall enough to be used for this purpose. He further ordered that the blossom 'shall be in the form of the cross and at the edge of each petal shall be the nail prints and in the center a crown of thorns.' And so it has been to this day."

"A Tree for All Seasons"
by John Wylie
Missouri Life, Volume 1, No. 1

TOUGH AND useful, beautiful and changeable with each season, making the best of what's at hand, and creating its own special place among its own kind bigger and better known . . . that's the dogwood, fittingly Missouri's state tree.

Growing on mostly hardscrabble soil, the dogwood reaches for the sun from undergrowth of taller trees, overwhelming entire forests with its showy whiteness against the still-bare trees of spring.

But its beauty comes not from the inconspicuous flowers but from the four waxy petals, a foursome of bracts which spray white layers before the leaves come on.

Beneath its beauty, the wood is practically indispensable to the textile industry. Hard and smooth and shock-resistant, it makes ideal weaving shuttles, not wearing the thread and becoming smoother the more it's used. The same qualities endear it to makers of golf clubs and mallets, wedges and jewelers' blocks.

Delicate of blossom and tough of wood, smallish and humble in name, distinctive . . . that's the dogwood.

On an overcast day, the dogwood's ethereal white floats among the woods of the Mark Twain National Forest along Route 32 near Bixby in Iron County.

*". . . Within eighteen months he had conquered it
and was one of the best pilots on the river."*

Albert Bigelow Paine
The Favorite Works of Mark Twain
Garden City Publishing Co., Inc., 1939

T OM!"
No answer.
"Tom!"
No answer.
"What's gone with that boy, I wonder? You TOM!"
No answer . . .

That was how it started—the beginning of *The Adventures of Tom Sawyer*, the greatest beginning ever written to any American novel, Ernest Hemingway called it.

And it was the beginning of a never-ending journey by peoples from all over the world to see where it happened, this eternal story of an eternal boyhood. From the fabric of his growing up and a fertile imagination, Mark Twain created Tom Sawyer in 1876. And with it, he put Hannibal, Missouri, forever on the map of the world.

The Mississippi was already there. But ever since "that boy" they've been coming, boy and man, woman and girl, to this old town by the river. They come to look and wander, to see and wonder, to be reminded as adults, as cagey old Sam Clemens wanted them to be, ". . . of what they once were themselves, and of how they felt and thought and talked, and what queer enterprises they sometimes engaged in."

He'd still recognize many of his old haunts and boyhood home, despite its well-kept garb, unusual in his day. But Sam wouldn't know his town—a bustling "city" now of some twenty thousand souls, with a cleaned-up waterfront area and Main Street—dotted with antique shops and old bookstores and similar tourist attractions, but with flavor left from earlier days.

Mark Twain would know his Mississippi, though. But he'd wonder at the strange boats navigating its tricky waters. When it came to riverboat pilots, old Cap'n Bill Heckman of Hermann used to say, they separated the men from the boys at the mouth of the Missouri: the boys went up the Mississippi and the men went up the Missouri.

But nowadays it's men only who pilot the towboats that push the barges up and down the Mississippi, under the nose of Mark's statue high up on the Pettibone bluffs, now Riverview Park. No ornate steamboats, the barges, flat and stout, carry thousands of tons of chemicals, grain, oil—basic bulk commodities to feed a nation's people and its industry, a nation of the likes to strain even Mark Twain's imaginative powers.

But the river they ply is still the same, flowing on downstream, past beautiful old Louisiana and Clarksville, Elsberry and Annada and Foley and Winfield. And these Lincoln Hills, as the geologists call them, look mostly the same from the river, where Mark Twain saw them in his day—except for a few changes like a cement plant and, "What in tarnation!", a lock and dam at Clarksville.

And these hills never lose the river for long. Through them and over them, Highway 79 rolls in a succession of unexpected beauties, curve after curve, hill after hill, with good flat farmland in between the broken bluffs, some pastured, some wooded. And off scenic pull-outs are views of the land, flat and fertile, to Illinois. And always the river . . .

Sometimes geography alone will insure a region's historic importance or its lasting pull on a people. Sometimes one person will do it.

Along the Mississippi, Mark Twain's river, the two came together.

*Samuel Langhorne Clemens
1835—Mark Twain—1910*

*His religion was humanity
and a whole world
mourned for him
when he died
Erected by
The State of Missouri
—1913—*

*Frederick C. Hibbard
Sculptor*

Below Hannibal's Riverview Park, Turtle Island still parts the broad Mississippi, and the river still lures young boys (of all ages and sexes), and boats still ride its waters—"towboats" pushing lines of barges carrying goods to feed and fuel a nation.

Mississippi

"The river," Magnolia had said, over
and over. "The river. The river."

Edna Ferber
Show Boat
International Collector's Library, 1926

"Cardiff Hill, beyond the village and above it . . .
lay just far enough away to seem a Delectable Land,
reposeful, and inviting."

Mark Twain
The Adventures of Tom Sawyer
Garden City Publishing Co., Inc., 1939

The lighthouse atop Cardiff Hill today is a beacon for tourists, not river
pilots seeking a guiding beam. They make the steep climb after soaking up the
shenanigans of Tom and Huck by wandering through Aunt Polly's gleaming
white frame house just a hop, skip and a jump toward town from the statue of
Twain's not-completely fictional boys.

At Louisiana, downstream from Hannibal, school children pause on the
way home long enough to pose for their picture. The old river town is home of
Stark's Bro's Nurseries, one of the largest, and the most famous apple tree
"builder," in the world.

Between Louisiana and Hannibal, Highway 79 dips and climbs
through the hills and fields bor-
dering the Mississippi, opening up
scenery that makes Pike Coun-
tians "Pshaw" the more-publi-
cized Ozarks.

North of Louisiana, pumpkins,
"For Sale," brighten the front
yard of one of the area's solid old
farm homes, now a family nur-
sery and garden center.

On a drizzly autumn day,
leaves glow softly like low candles, lighting the woods of the
Dupont Reservation on one of the
many scenic lookouts along Route
79 south of Hannibal.

"For sixty years the foreign tourist has steamed up and down the river between St. Louis and New Orleans, and then gone home and written his book; believing he had seen all of the river that was worth seeing . . . ."

Mark Twain
Life on the Mississippi
Garden City Publishing Co. Inc., 1939

"It's a bit damp," but the soybeans must be harvested around Laddonia on Route 54. And it's "keep rolling" this morning for the Illinois Central Gulf freight through Vandalia, farming and fire brick and clay center.

At Clarksville, a stately home ushers travelers on Route W and WW into panoramic miles of other well-kept houses amid rolling farmlands. And at Louisiana, The River moodily makes way for an upbound towboat, slipping under the Champ Clark Bridge to Illinois.

In the Gasconade Hills

". . . Steep bluffs, gorgeous cuts, hairpin turns, and lazy eddies; hardwoods, softwoods and dogwoods . . . four-legged creatures quenching their thirst at water's edge, while listless white clouds float above. . . ."

"The Gasconade"
The Rivers of Missouri
Missouri Conservation Commission, 1953

YOU CAN see the weather coming up here," Bill Sims had told me. "Mostly, from those far ridges—time enough to head for the house or the barn. And watch."

There was much to watch in those hills, with an unending view of receding ridges that gave a man an up-here-all-alone feeling, on top of his own private world.

Occasionally, Wilbur would rattle by in his old pickup truck on his way to the river. And Lance would jog by trailed by old Gus.

But mostly the old Pointer farm was a haven of seclusion and quiet, a perfect place to work, I thought . . .

But there were hummingbirds to watch in the columbines by the back porch—hovering to take split-second nips of the nectar; dive-bombing would-be invaders; flying flashy courtships in perfectly executed figure eights to dazzle their lady loves . . .

And the bluebirds came, first one, then a second brilliant male, checking out the little house on the fence post—but apparently unable to overcome "her" objections to the nearby LP gas tank . . .

From the dining room window, in the thorn-thick field toward the highway, I could see a trio of wild turkeys wandering in late afternoon, feeding fearlessly, almost disdainfully . . . after the hunting season.

And along about dusk, bobbing along the ridgeline atop a long draw, I might see heads of deer on their way to feed or to bed down.

And there was always the garden. It grew

A morning river of April fog fills the valleys between the ridges of hills stretching from the old Pointer barn toward Mt. Sterling on Route 50, eight miles away.

The rusty plow awaits a pusher in the garden by the old garage and the new apple tree.

luxuriant—full of Bill's broccoli and cabbage; lettuce, three kinds; radishes, red and white; carrots, long and yellow, tiny and tasty.

The two cherry trees, too, in the far corner of the garden out by the old barn, attracted their share of attention and action, the birds homing in early on the bright yellows and reds of the ripening fruit that finally filled both trees to heavy laden. Even after Bill and Betty and the birds finished picking their fill, there were cherries a-plenty for some remembering pies . . .

The days ended all too soon, tumbling into weeks. And I quit trying to tally up the amount of actual work accomplished during those two months on the old Pointer place. It seemed unimportant, after a while.

I never asked Bill how much land I "owned" for those two months. I think it was four or five hundred acres, or thereabouts.

But it didn't really matter. I was rich. It seemed like the whole world.

Some of the old homes in the hills
are empty now. But by the side
porch, spirea still thrives and
sweet william still blooms.

Like a setting from "Briga-
doon," Cooper Hill nestles in its
own little valley "behind" Mt.
Sterling. And the church, midway
down the hill, welcomes all.

". . . And where you can watch as I did last evening
twelve deer browse unafraid in a little glade.

Thad Snow
From Missouri
Houghton Mifflin Company, 1954

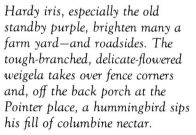

Hardy iris, especially the old
standby purple, brighten many a
farm yard—and roadsides. The
tough-branched, delicate-flowered
weigela takes over fence corners
and, off the back porch at the
Pointer place, a hummingbird sips
his fill of columbine nectar.

*On the hillsides and along the "crick," pastures "green up"
with the freshness of spring; the side garden, fortified and
enriched with load after load of turkey manure (there's
plenty of it from the many raisers nearby), grows lush from
soft showers. And out by the barn the Michigan sour-pitted
cherry tree loads itself to drooping.*

"Entirely within Missouri, the river winds nearly 300 miles from its source near Hartville to the Missouri River, an airline distance of about 120 miles."

Oz Hawksley
Missouri Ozark Waterways
Missouri Conservation Commission, 1965

Booksack in hand, mother and daughter meet the Thomas Jefferson Library Bookmobile at its stop at the old Langenberg Store, now an antique shop, at Hope, a few miles north of Freedom.

At Gasconade, a "retired" dredge boat stands by as the winding river empties—finally—into the waiting Missouri.

Weston and Up North

SOUTH OF "downtown," past the Pepper, Kisker, Pepper tobacco warehouses, Main Street of Weston crosses the weedy railroad tracks and disappears, forgetting where the river went.

Once, the Missouri flowed here, twenty feet deep, where the two warehouses sprawl. Early settlers docked here, on their way to reap riches from the Platte Purchase land. Steamboats tied up here to load on tobacco for shipment downriver to Glasgow and St. Louis. And Weston was "The Queen of the Steamboat Days."

Gradually, the river shifted its course, leaving Weston three miles away. The steamboats disappeared, the overland freight and stagecoach business waned and the railroads moved north and south.

But tobacco stayed, and each November until the last "hand" is sold the warehouses echo with the auctioneer's chant and the big trucks roll into town to haul out the huge compressed bales. And Weston is . . . still Weston.

It's an anomaly . . . a country town, half-hidden in a little valley squeezed between Missouri River bluffs—thirty-odd miles northeast of Kansas City and fifteen minutes from jet-modern Kansas City International Airport.

It's a busy, working town, with mud and dirt on its streets, a trade center for local farmers and agri-businesses. And it's a tourist town, with scores of historic antebellum homes perched on its hilly streets.

Like Weston, the road into it hasn't changed much, except it's blacktop now. Off the whizz and whine of Interstate 29, through Platte City, Route J heads west . . . generally. Even smooth-surfaced, it's a slow-down road,

following the line of least resistance across or along little valleys and climbing the abrupt hills when it must.

The road runs through a scenic countryside of loping hills and fields full of after-harvest stubble—tobacco and milo stalks and soybean rubble. And in nearby orchards, regiments of apple trees in burnished golds and browns march through still-green grass into the distance.

Cattle munch contentedly in churned-black feedlots, and pigs wallow joyously in their element. The whole country, it seems, was made to produce—and so it does, in abundance and variety.

Early on a mid-November morning, an Up North chill swept the hilltops around Weston. But the sun shone warmly on headstones of a little cemetery at the edge of an orchard.

Six small markers, lined up in a row, told a stark story: six infants from one family had died and been buried here. None had lived beyond six months—mute evidence, it seemed that morning, of the rigors of life on this land, of the hard work to make it productive, of the personal price the pioneers paid for making this home.

But the land produced, and the people survived. And Weston itself outlived the heydays of steamboats, the halcyon era of rich Ben Holladay and the stagecoach lines—and the passing of all of them.

Today it remembers its sometimes turbulent, sometimes glory-filled past. It remembers the people and the places of its century and a half, and it endures.

Weston cherishes its quiet and peacefulness away from the din of the city. And today they call it "The Quiet Queen."

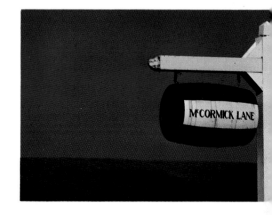

Major David Holladay started the nation's oldest operating distillery in 1856 when he found out that the limestone spring waters near his mill made ideal Bourbon whiskey—and more money than his mill.

"The Eden of the American continent," one writer called Weston. It was the first city in the Platte Purchase, a $7,500 plus livestock deal with Indians for two million acres of rich land that rounded out present Missouri boundaries.

"It's darn hard work, but it pays good. And once you get it in your blood, you can't get away from it."

Tobacco farmer
"Tobacco Time in Weston"
Missouri Life
Volume 5, No. 4

Hull's Burley Acres, home of a family synonymous with tobacco, dominates the last hilltop on the road into Weston.

The father of George Z. Hull, one of several brothers growing and selling tobacco, came to Weston from Kentucky because the land there "was worn out by 1895." Fertilizers, Hull says, "make the difference" for today's tobacco farmers.

Corn, wheat and soybeans, and apples—Weston farmers grow them, too, in addition to tobacco. Such crops take far fewer man-hours from seedbed to harvest.

Harvested around Labor Day, the tobacco goes to the warehouse for auctioning, which runs from late November until the crop is sold, usually in late January. In a good year about six million tons are sold as buyers from the major tobacco companies flock to Weston, the only such auction west of the Mississippi.

*"It's corn and cattle country, country where the winds of
winter pile snowdrifts high enough to hide a man, country that
the glacier gave back grudgingly and grindingly."*

Roy Stoneman
"Route 36: Road for a Sturdy People"
Missouri Highways June-July 1971

Most of the apples have been picked, and the tobacco hanging in the big white barn will soon be
hauled into town. But on its highest hill, surrounded by rolling acres of Vaughan's Orchard's apple
trees, headstones of an old cemetery stand out
starkly against an early morning sky in November.

Tobacco barns, with their narrow, vertical
doors, sit on the crests of many hills around Weston. During damp weather, the farmers open the
doors so the leaves can absorb moisture and become leathery, or "in case."

But all doors are shut tight in winter here and
along Route 36 east of St. Joseph in Buchanan
County, in the Up North Country where man and
beast live with the worst of Missouri winter . . .
first.

Arcadia...and Around

The countryside is still peaceful, here near Black in the "wilds" of Reynolds County. But, underground, record productions of zinc, lead and iron are revitalizing the area's economy.

It was a real, honest-to-goodness general store at Bixby, where Routes 32 and 49 cross paths. And the owner was genuinely general-store friendly, as he nodded at the yard across the road.

"Mom'd be real proud that you're taking pictures of her tulips," he said. "This drizzle won't help any though, will it?"

"YOU SHOULD see it when the hoarfrost is on the mountains," Cal Dothage had said. But the Arcadia Valley is "show 'em" country any time, an elongated pocket some ten miles long and a couple wide, utterly unlike any place in Missouri. And if I can find someone who hasn't seen it, I itch to take them there.

But I wondered if the Valley had changed.

Driving south down Highway 21, I felt "it" coming on at Caledonia, still clustered along the banks of Goose Creek at the "gate" to Bellevue Valley; then stronger through Graniteville and those Elephant Rocks, still curious and still humorous; then . . . Pilot Knob and the ruins of Fort Davidson.

It all looked the same.

The valley floor spread flat and wide, swallowing the highway down its middle as it reached for Pilot Knob and Iron and Shepherd mountains at its far rims.

Somehow, "mountains" fits these hills, although Taum Sauk, Missouri's tallest, over in the mist is only 1,772 feet high. Perhaps it's the vista—the expanse of the Valley abruptly halted by knobs and peaks jutting abruptly upward, forested and hazy blue in the distance. Or maybe it's their age, demanding respect and veneration for their toughness, their enduring for more than a billion years.

They hadn't changed a whit since the last time I saw them. I was proud of them.

It was spring, and the dogwood floated ghostly white in the woods, against the oaks and hickories and occasional ashes, still stark and black with the dampness of a recent shower.

But there were some changes.

New houses dotted the level land and edged farther up into the mountains. And the farms looked bigger, most of them.

At Ironton the sun came out, showing off the old courthouse's new coat of iron-ish red and pristine white trim. But the sun bedded down early, hurrying our looks at the old homes with a feeling of night's cold—and warming hopes for the fragile hoarfrost, born of sudden, overnight changes of temperature invading the valley.

But morning dawned to a drizzle, and mist hung, becoming, on the hills.

Down through Royal Gorge, the highway and its granite guardwall still clung to the ledge above the boulder-strewn creek tumbling below. And on down Highway 49 the towns still called out their colorful names: Hogan, Glover, Chloride, Sabula, Annapolis, Vulcan and Des Arc . . . and Gads Hill, a railroad sign off the road, where Jesse James and his gang pulled off the first train robbery in Missouri.

We veered off northwest, then, on the back side of Taum Sauk, into Iron County still—not the Valley, but hilly and forested, mile on mile. And underneath it lay the Viburnum Trend.

Precambrian old but newly-discovered and tapped deep, the Trend underlies much of this region. And down there in it men were at work in some of the world's newest and biggest and deepest mines. But except for an occasional opening in the thick woods, a sign and a road leading back into some new mill, there was little indication of the new day come to this old land of mountains.

As in Arcadia, the dogwood gleamed over here—ghostly white, too, in the morning drizzle. There was a newness in this place, but one that was guarding well the old, still changeless despite all its years.

More new mornings would come here, and there would be a morning when the hoarfrost silvered the mountains, over there guarding the Valley.

And we'd be back.

The immaculate, iron-red courthouse, with its simple lines and
Greek-Revival cornices and entrance, was built in 1858. It was
used as a refuge by retreating
Union troops after about 1,000
of them defeated General Sterling
Price's "last-ditch" army of
12,000 in September of 1864 at
Fort Davidson.

". . . He could do the area justice only were he to live there for many months and explore the mountains, the shut-ins, and many other features on foot."

Thomas R. Beveridge
"Mountains, Hills, Knobs & Mounds"
Geologic Wonders and Curiosities of Missouri
Missouri Division of Geology and Land Survey, 1978

Sidewalk tulips riot in front of the old-fashioned gazebo on the courthouse lawn in Ironton.

And spirea sprays green and white underneath some wrought iron handiwork of John Haefner behind the "William T. Gay Home," now owned by the Haefners.

Big Sugar Country

It's an "in the bones" kind of place, a place where a man can tarry a spell . . . or a lifetime.

And they come here, to the Big Sugar Country, for reasons as varied as they are.

From West Virginia young Bill Atkinson moved in because "the hills are pretty, a lot like the mountains back home, only not so high. But they've got more 'coons."

His younger sister, Debbie, came and saw and agreed . . . and stayed.

George Foster decided to chuck his construction business in Tulsa and bought the venerable Ginger Blue Resort on Elk River.

Don O'Brien is "homegrown," a native of Pineville. And he stays here—to run a spread-out operation that overflows into the valleys of Big Sugar Creek and Elk River and out onto the flatlands west toward Oklahoma with fine quarter horses, Limousin beef cattle, chicken hatcheries and processing plants.

And Don Walker ramrods Crag O'Lea Resort, hefting canoes and renting his hillside "close to nature" cabins to escape the hectic pace of a Hollywood publicist.

I come down here as often as I can . . . to touch ground that is still open, to walk in woods that feel virgin and primeval, to wade in glass-clear water and watch the suckers lazing in the current, to float silently on the river and see blue herons on their spindly stilt-legs feeding in the shallows, to spy on a herd of deer floating in morning mist along the willows at water's edge, to doze drowsily listening to crows cawing, high in the sky on a summer afternoon.

Mostly, it's quiet country—except for that summer of '38 when "Jesse James" roared in.

Tyrone Power, Henry Fonda, Nancy Kelly and Jane Darwell and Henry King and their entourage poured into these hills and valleys to make one of Hollywood's first big "on location" films.

They spread dirt on Pineville's four paved streets, put false fronts on the stores, offered mouth-gaping farmers twenty dollars a day just to let a posse chase Jesse across their fields. They generally caromed around the countryside, and left McDonald County in a dusty haze that the people recreate around every Fourth of July during "Jesse James Days," showing the old movie over and over and reminiscing about "Remember when. . . ."

But Big Sugar is far from a "remember when" country. For the Atkinsons, the Fosters, the O'Briens, the Walkers—and their few thousand neighbors—it's home.

They may drive miles to work — to Rocketdyne or Lazy-Boy or Lindsay up at Neosho, or on to Atlas or FAG or Eagle-Picher at Joplin. Or down to Bentonville, where Wal-Mart "gives fits" to the nation's retail giants.

But they come back home to Big Sugar's away-from-it-all beauty, the clear waters, the woods and the ravines of Huckleberry Ridge Forest. They fish and float Indian Creek and the two Sugars and Elk River. They hunt deer and chase 'coons to the holler-filling bawlings of tough, rangy coonhounds.

And they live the good life, here on this land that remains scenic, with its sleeves rolled up.

At least, that's what I see each time I go back . . . and how I remember it, in my bones, until then.

And I hope it never changes.

Across the valley, outside a still-sturdy log cabin, a lone horse waits, pensively, as if for his master, too long inside.

Penitentiary Ridge, where two bandits were cornered and sent off to prison, overlooks a green thumb of land formed by a sweeping curve of Big Sugar flowing, within a mile and a half, in all directions except north.

It's empty now, and they don't gather here anymore at Jane but, ah, the tales that once were swapped here.

At the Mt. Shira pull-off south of Ginger Blue, early-rising youngsters climb on the bus for a long ride to the "new" school at Anderson.

The watchers quietly eye passersby on the road to Cyclone east of Pineville.

"Joe Schell called this Big Sugar Country a 'legendary paradise.' To my thinking, he's not far off."

Charlie Edmonds
Missouri Life
Volume 1, No. 2

*In Noel, "at the bridge," Harry and Catherine Cantrell run the Ozark Origins antique shop, backed up on Shadow Lake and, over on Highway 59, the area's famous overhanging bluffs.
The dining room at Ginger Blue Resort overlooks beautiful Elk River—with its hordes of sunning turtles and, sometimes in early morning, deer feeding on the far bank.*

"Sometimes I wish all of us down here—me, too—would just be quiet; then we could keep all of this to ourselves. But we won't. It's too good not to talk about."

Don Walker
Owner, Crag O'Lea Resort
Pineville

Like quaking aspen in early evening light, a stand of sycamores line the creek bank along Route H, between Pineville and Noel.

At Cyclone, Big Sugar spills over an old mill dam in velvet sheets in its hurry to join Elk River. Overshadowed as a whitewater canoeing stream, the Big Sugar is rated a II by Dr. Oz Hawksley on the difficulty scale, compared to the renowned Current River's rating of I.

In a creek pasture near Powell some "new" Limousin cattle graze. And "proud cattle," they are, says Debbie Atkinson. "They're alert and watch every move you make."

FROM TOP
Counterclockwise

Katherine Hamilton
Lover of life, Dittmer

Jim Spencer
Railroad man, Vandalia

John Travis
Cattleman, Lebanon

Charlie Wiess
Raconteur, Retired
Barnett

Lowell Davis
Artist, Carthage

Aloys Eisenratt
Jolly Deutschlander
Rhineland

Rebecca O'Hanlon
Writer and digger
Jefferson City

CENTER

Opal Meador
Bonnet lover
Shell Knob

Missouri is . . .
Its People

Frona and Others

I WAS twenty-six years old when I came to Joplin to take over the old
Worth Hotel . . . . It was a wild, wide-open town . . . .
"Now, looking back, it might not seem like just the best place in
the world for someone like me to go. I was a young widow with three
children. I was also a beautiful young woman—the kind men loved to
pinch.

"On top of that, I was little. But I figured I was smart enough to take
care of myself. Besides, my grandfather always said if you want the biggest
job done the best, pick out the littlest woman you can find and let 'er go."

Frona Norman
"The Joplin I Knew"
Missouri Life
Volume 1, No. 1

Kelly Nunn
Hit of family reunion
Morrisville

". . . All callers always received the bouquet and more, because it was Miss Molly's pleasure to share her beautiful blooms."

Jake Heggie
"Azalea Time in Charleston"
Missouri Life
Volume 7, No. 1

In April, Charleston becomes a showplace of blooming beauty during its Dogwood-Azalea Festival.

"The City of Beautiful Homes" is the county seat of Mississippi County, Missouri's easternmost county, encircled by the river. Bird's Point at its edge lies slightly east of Bloomington, in central Illinois.

Small Town, Missouri, U.S.A.

THE WORLD had been made "safe" again. My Navy discharge papers—July 16, 1946—were in my pocket. The Frisco's *Texas Flyer* was rolling southwest out of St. Louis, and I felt as if I'd never have another worry in the world. I was going home.

Out of the train's clickety rhythm, I remembered that summer twelve years before. We didn't know it then, but it was a summer of change—a precursor of many summers and winters of change that would sweep the world. Now, like the scenes glimpsed from the train window, memories of that first time away from home ran through my mind . . .

It was "drouthy" again that summer of '34, and the garden burned to a crisp—again—so we took a "vacation."

I don't remember much about the place now —a small, white frame house with a screened-in back porch, a rundown barn leaning tiredly in a feedlot full of hard-dried thistles and horseweeds, a brown-singed pasture that crunched under bare feet, a stream that still trickled warm pools beyond the row of hedge apple trees. But that year it was Timbuktu, Shangri-La and all of the exotic, exciting places of the world rolled into one fascinating corner of Missouri.

For four whole days we were there, at Fred and Serena's farm on Cowskin Branch, a few miles east of Goodman. That's nine miles south of Neosho, by the main highway, and it's eight miles west of Granby. So we were a long, long way from home.

*"The early people came from hilly Normandy
. . . with their hats, clothes, a handful of grapes
and apple seeds. . . ."*

Sarah Morris

I was seven, going on eight; Lyle was just ten. Ma was forty-four. And Cowskin was the farthest away from home I'd ever been—and the first time for "overnight."

Until that summer, home and all of its small-town wonders were world enough for any wide-eyed, barefooted boys in overalls. Down the road a few skips—close enough to claim as our very own private domain—loomed mountainous "tailin' piles," great, lumpy mounds of acidic "chat," residue from the lead mills that once scrunched and crushed, shook and sluiced the heavy lead from the rocks hauled up from underground mines whose shafts still pockmarked the countryside.

Lead had made Granby a boom town once—and enlivened it again when World War II needed it. As the water tank on the Highway 60 hill proudly announced, it was "The Oldest Mining Town in the Southwest."

Founded in 1850, it had threatened briefly, around the turn of the century, to outstrip Joplin as a rip-roaring, wide-open town, born of riches dug from the red clay and rocks of this tri-state area where Missouri, Kansas and Oklahoma butt together. But in the thirties it was a "typical" small town, if any place with that background—particularly in Missouri—could be typical.

To hear the old-timers tell it, the whole town, and for miles around it, was undershot with tunnels and penetrated by deep shafts from which the lead and zinc and "jack" had been dynamited and gouged by pick and shovel. And, "One of these days, sure's I'm sittin' here, the

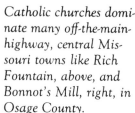

Catholic churches dominate many off-the-main-highway, central Missouri towns like Rich Fountain, above, and Bonnot's Mill, right, in Osage County.

And each town boasts of a "fine home" or two, like this "Kingston house" at Granby in Newton County.

"What remains is a picturesque, story-book village whose people continue to enjoy the simple pleasures of life."

Sarah Morris
"Bonnot's Mill"
Missouri Life
Volume 2, No. 3

*Festivals, flowers, fruit . . . they still bloom
with Fall in small towns and along the
"old" two-lane roads.*

whole shebang's gonna fall in."

That made a plenty adventuresome place to grow up in—what with all the danger and discovery that imaginative young minds could add to the stories.

We lived at the edge of town, halfway up the last hill on the "old road" to Neosho, the county seat and the "next big town." It was "lease land," rented from the Federal Mining and Smelting Company which owned much of the area and retained all mineral rights to it until the fifties. But the "improvements" were ours—the house, the smokehouse and chicken house, the new garage and the Pa-made barn backed into a hillside. And we owned the shaft dumps, overgrown with thickets of paradise trees, gooseberry bushes, hawthorns, and wild cherry trees hanging full of tantalizing 'possum grapes.

Exposed by long-abandoned and "jacked-out" diggin's, our very own cave led down and under the back "rock patch," alternately a poorish kind of pasture with thin stands of lespedeza or red clover, or a corn field that burned up sooner than most. But it was always a place of solitude, out of sight over a shaft dump from the house, and a haven for rabbits which occasionally stumbled over the rocks to give a fair chance to a kid with a single shot rifle.

Up the hill where town petered out, the hay prairie took over, toward even smaller towns like Newtonia and Stark City, and Boulder City and Stella. And far away south were Pineville and Lanagan and Noel, where the tourists came.

Down north, Main Street dropped off the last hill and wandered without a name for two dusty

*Ginger Blue's annual arts and crafts show features
such variety as a nylon-stocking "Kitchen Witch"
and a time-consuming Cathedral Window quilt.*

*Mt. Vernon's "Apple Butter Days" include blue
ribbons for most authentic costumes—and the fun
of watching a crosscut sawing contest.*

*And the yard at Choctaw and Broadway in
Southwest City goes on a wild-blooming warpath
. . . while it's apple time at Gray's Orchard stand
near Republic.*

"They bring the products of their skill to county fairs . . . from field and orchard and barnlot and housewife's kitchen."
Irving Dilliard
Missouri: A Guide to the Show-Me State
Duell, Sloan & Pearce, 1941

"Take a picture of the young'uns, the handsome ones," Mr. Peters said proudly. "And my pretty granddaughter."

miles to Shoal Creek, goggle-eyed and bullhead-ish and channel catfish-ish, curving along and under the Frisco tracks that connected distant places like Tulsa and St. Louis.

Joplin, twenty-eight miles away, was "The City"—with swaying overhead lights that changed colors to govern the flow of traffic. And there was plenty. Cattle trucks and pickups, hay trucks and dump trucks, locals and long-haulers, and fancy cars flowed in and through the city, all awesome to a small town boy.

They came, grownups said, from just about everywhere—traveling new concrete pavements, like Highway 71 from Des Moines and St. Joseph and Kansas City all the way south to New Orleans, and Route 66, following the old Osage Trail from the Southwest up to St. Louis on the Mississippi . . . and beyond even, they said, to the fabled city of Chicago.

They were place-names in daydreams on summer days . . . after the garden was hoed and weeded. Or at night, lying still and alone among big brothers and sisters on an old comfort or quilt in the front yard, watching stars wink through the old cedars.

Often, after supper, we'd visit relatives or neighbors—Uncle Sherd and Aunt Fannie Howard, small and tilting forward with years and an eagerness to be kind to everyone, especially "young'uns"; Uncle John Shewmake and Annie, for an evening of oft-told stories of the run to Oklahoma—and the hurry back when Pa Stoneman quickly decided that it was "for the Indians"; Bill and Molly Miller, back home after a working life in the oil fields of west Texas; and

Granddaughter, and dog
Near Taos

The Capitol
"No more imposing edifice"
Jefferson City

The Gospel Tones
Prairie Home

The Monaco Home
Jefferson City

"They sang the songs their grandparents used to sing on Sunday afternoons . . . . simple, down-to-earth music."

"In the Key of B for Bluegrass"
Bittersweet Country
Anchor Press/Doubleday, 1978

"The White House disclosed today . . . Chur-
chill will discuss 'world affairs' in an address at
Westminster College, March 5 (1946)."

Virgil Johnston
"Sir Winston Comes to Fulton"
Missouri Life, Volume 1, No. 3

the Fullers, moved in from Arkansas with a
lively load of tales of railroading and life in the
hills around Mena—and an old-gold Stromberg-
Carlson table radio that never missed Major
Bowes and His Amateur Hour, the Grand Ol'
Opry, nor Fibber McGee and Molly . . .

Sometimes we'd drop off to sleep on the floor
to the drone of adult talk; then awake and
stumble back home to bed.

Across the road from Fullers', we often
jangled the screen door "announcin'" bell at
Nichols' Grocery, long and narrow and full of
wondrous delights. And Gladys or Naomi were
soft touches for neighborhood kids, handing out
an all-day sucker or a Hershey bar for a boyish
song and dance.

Saturday night meant buying the "main"
groceries downtown and visiting on the
streets—and maybe listening, in the back of
Darnell's Grocery, to Cal Jefferson and pickers
and fiddlers with forgotten names playing as
long as there was anyone left in town.

Under the benevolent dictatorship of Super-
intendent H.W. Smith, school was a no-non-
sense dose of the Three R's, with few "electives"
and no frills. Church, at the First Baptist, the
largest of some two dozen congregations among
sixteen hundred people, was twice on Sunday,
morning and evening, and prayer meeting on
Wednesday—if Ma insisted.

It was a cozy, comfortable world, this Small
Town growing-up place—even during the De-
pression—a close-knit world of home and
church, school and work, relatives and family.
Perhaps, looking back now, it all sounds too

The Churchill Memorial includes a library, a
museum and art gallery—underneath the ancient church of St. Mary, Aldermanbury,
shipped stone-by-stone from England and
reassembled on the site—all in commemora-
tion of the historic "Iron Curtain" speech.

In Morgan County, "behind" nearby peo-
ple-packed Lake of the Ozarks—and decades
from Gasper's—a young Mennonite couple
bundles up for a Sunday afternoon buggy
ride.

"We may doze but we never close," boasts Gasper's at King-
dom City where Interstate 70 and Route 54 cross. And daily,
by the hundreds, the truckers roll in, to doze and eat, to fill up
and roll on—making it Missouri's largest, and one of the
nation's busiest, truck stops.

94

"There's something special about the quality of life in Missouri—with its famous variety extending to recreational, cultural and life-style characteristics."

Missouri: Facts and Figures
Missouri Tourism Commission, 1981

idyllic, too much the conjurings of a selective memory, too much a distillation of good times from harsh realities.

But those came soon enough.

Seven years after that Cowskin summer, World War II exploded over it, Small Town and The City. Much of Cowskin flowed through land encompassed by sprawling, soldier-packed Camp Crowder, one of the major Signal Corps bases in the nation. And a whole nation of wide-eyed boys and young men—and women—saw more of the world than they could ever have imagined.

They changed the world, and they changed. And The City they came back to changed. And so did Small Town.

But, still, not far away from anywhere, somewhere at the far end of a pasture, beyond some row of hedge apples, a Cowskin still flows with a trickle of new discovery.

In Boone County, part of "Little Dixie," new homes match old mansions for gracious living, only minutes away from Columbia, the home of the University of Missouri and Stephens and Columbia colleges.

Looping across hill and valley, REA lines bring electric living to rural homes—and places of worship like the Berger Church in Gasconade County.

And at the edge of Blackwater, near Arrow Rock, small town gardeners still plant gladiolus for "pretty" and dill for pickles.

They still breed fine saddle horses around Mexico, and it's still the center of one of the world's most important fire-clay areas. And it still combines modernity and tradition—and fine houses like the Bond home on the A.P. Green Estate.

"Missouri is and always has been more tidy in its rural areas (excepting the true hill country) than the nearby southern states."

MacKinlay Kantor
Missouri Bittersweet
Doubleday & Company, Inc., 1969

"We're trying to show what private funding can do to save the inner city."

Donald Hall, President
Hallmark Cards, Inc.

Missouri is . . .
Its People

Donald Hall

IT'S ONE of few family-owned and family-run corporate leaders remaining in the United States. And the Halls of Hallmark—founder and father Joyce and president and son Donald—are private people who prefer a personal family life out of the limelight, happy to let their deeds and products speak for themselves.

But they keep doing things on a scale that makes attention inevitable . . . world-wide.

Like Hallmark Cards, Inc. . . .

On six continents and in dozens of languages, "For those who care enough to send the very best" speaks of high quality, assured. And it is believed.

And under its banner more than a thousand men and women, in a globe-girdling complex of affiliates and subsidiaries, sell Hallmark greeting cards, gift wrapping, party accessories, books, stationery, candles, ribbons, puzzles, pens and pencils and dozens of other "social expression" products.

Like the Hallmark Hall of Fame . . .

On television this superb dramatic series tells consumers about "the very best"—and the industry rewards the company for its high attainments with forty-nine coveted Emmy awards, filling a room at Hallmark headquarters in another attention-getter . . . Like Crown Center . . .

This "city-within-a-city" bespeaks a half-billion dollar Hallmark belief in the future, with new answers to old urban problems.

Crown Center covers one hundred acres near downtown Kansas City. Planned for eight thousand permanent residents and a daytime population of fifty thousand, it's within a couple of minutes of the downtown freeway loop—with offices, theaters, shops, hotels, parks and residences. And all built for people, by people who care enough to build the very best.

These are the things which talk for Hallmark. But Donald Hall talks—forcefully and expressively—about this place where it lives and does business:

"We wanted to bring new business to Kansas City, to Missouri . . .

"Our Midwest area has so much to offer in the way of geographic centrality, in communications and distribution economics.

"Hallmark has conducted a national and international business from Kansas City for seventy-two years. Other firms could, too.

"We have done everything we know how to design a 'city-within-a-city' for people. It is the human environment that concerns us most."

Like his father, Donald Hall continues Kansas City's traditional "legacy of leadership," strong from its early days. On it they have stamped their own uncompromising allegiance to quality, a rare concern for their employees and the quality of life within the company they direct—and in the city where its home is.

And where they live, as privately as such hallmarks will allow.

"New York has fountains and so has Rome, but Kansas City is deluged with them."
Herbert Silverman
Travel and Leisure

It started here, at the Country Club Plaza with the magnificent J. C. Nichols Memorial Fountain. And the city's fascination with bubbling waters is still erupting all over the metropolis. In the early seventies, private citizens raised $400,000 to build a fountain a year—for fifteen years.

"One of the loveliest . . ."

"I was thinking of moving it to Omaha, but a traveling cigar salesman said, 'Omaha is all right, but you want to go to Kansas City.' "

Joyce Hall
"Kansas City, Heartland, U.S.A."
National Geographic
July, 1976

"HAVE YOU seen Kansas City lately?" one traveling salesman asks another.

"Yes," replies the other. "I was there two weeks ago."

"Well," says the first one. "You should see it now!"

The story, altogether appropriate to this surprising city, is probably apocryphal. But perhaps not. It's the same city, after all, which saw, in five years, The Chicago Connection, The Coming of Turkey Red and The Dawn of the Twilight Twinkler.

With those three events, Kansas City assured its preeminence in the rich agricultural region where the Midwest farmlands merge into the Great Plains, it solidified its ranking as a major city in the United States, and it guaranteed a future description as "one of its loveliest."

But none of them came easy.

After the Civil War the nation, healing its wounds, looked West. And Independence, Westport, St. Joseph, Leavenworth, Lawrence—all were competing with Kansas City for dominance of the area.

The railroads were tracking west . . . but they needed a bridge across the Missouri. And in 1869, led by Robert Van Horn, the city grabbed the vital prize—the Hannibal Bridge. It made Kansas City the connecting link between the cattle country of the Southwest and the meat packing empires of Chicago.

She became the Queen of the Cowtowns. And, positioned between eastern manufacturers and the West's rapidly expanding markets, the Queen became one of the nation's leading distribution centers.

Turkey Red came in 1874, an "emigrant" from the Russian Crimea. "Red" was seed wheat, hard red winter wheat, brought into Kansas by

For lunch, study and romance, the Plaza offers convenient beauty to employees of nearby St. Luke's Hospital.

"It's a spirit that presumes problems can be solved . . . an attitude that regards a crisis as a challenge of grit and imagination."

Dr. Charles Kimball, Chairman
Midwest Research Institute

A sense of aesthetics—and the feel of affluence—mark the Kansas City "style," even to details of a stone wall, along with another fountain, this one forming a rainbow at Meyer Circle on Ward Parkway.

Off Ward Parkway, well-manicured lawns and fine homes line the side streets in both directions in one of the nation's most beautiful residential areas.

Mennonites forced to move from Russia, after leaving their German homeland to escape armed service conscription. Kansas City, in the early seventies, was growing as a grain marketing center . . . but there was nothing on any market like Turkey Red.

The hardy emigrant would evolve into hard winter wheat that would set a standard for bread wheat around the world. It made Kansas the greatest wheat producing state in the nation . . . and Kansas City became the marketing center for it—and for a host of other riches from the plains to the west.

"You couldn't get it done today," one historian later wrote of the job led by The Dawn of the Twilight Twinkler.

In 1872 "it" might have looked like a hopeless, pie-in-the-sky task. But, then, the sky was the limit for Kansas City, even in those days.

The city had grown from a wild and woolly frontier town into, as historian Lew Larkin described it, ". . . an ugly boom town, a cow town, a hilly town of muddy streets and sidewalks."

Audaciously enough, "it" was a movement to turn this into "The City Beautiful." It started with newspapers—the *Times* and the *Journal*, with irresistible impetus added by William Rockhill Nelson and his "Twilight Twinkler," as some called his *Star*.

And there were many more men who caught the vision of This City Beautiful . . .

"Cities are many things to many people, and Kansas City can be all those things with one essential quality assured—the quality of life."

Harald Peter
Kansas City
Hallmark Editions, 1973

Modern Alameda Plaza enhances the "old" of the Plaza district, and in River Quay, where the city began, rehabilitation tries to restore it anew.

Jesse Clyde Nichols looked out over the raw, unsightly Brush Creek Valley—marshy and weed-infested—and he saw the Country Club Plaza. He started building it in 1922, and it became the world's first shopping center . . . and much more.

Nichols's creed was "Create value where there is none." And, he would add with a grin, "And make it pay."

The Nichols credo and influence spread south and west from the Plaza, spilling over into the eastern prairies of Kansas, to put a distinctive, prestigious touch of its own on the total "City Beautiful."

Later the same Kansas City "style," the term borrowed and redirected from its jazz of Prohibition and Pendergast days, blossomed anew when the Halls—Joyce and Donald—created Crown Center, making unsightly Signboard Hill and its waterfall a centerpiece for a private development seldom seen in any city . . .

And so it still goes in Kansas City. So even if you saw it two weeks ago, you should see it now.

Sing
a Small
Song

A celebration to every day,
wherever it dawns

Foggy Bottom

"The road '. . . is a silent specta-
tor in the battle between man and
river . . . a continuous fight for
the land.'"

Bruce Mitchell
"The Winding Way to Yesterday"
Missouri Highways
December-January 1970-71

The Old Store

"God Bless Missouri, and I love
an old tick hound more than a
Japanese motorcycle, and a board-
ed-up crossroads store better than
W. T. Grant's, Katz', or Sears'."

MacKinlay Kantor
Missouri Bittersweet
Doubleday & Company, Inc., 1969

Rhineland Road

". . . A visa to the pastoral 'Rhine Valley' that its early German settlers found so homelike."

Al Foster
"The New Rhine Road"
Missouri Life
Volume 1, No. 3

Osage Morning

The air crept in, cool, encompass-
ing, and in the broad valleys it
met yesterday's warm waters,
bathing the river of the Osages in
misty shrouds.

Ma's Iris

*"Sometimes I wish I could re-
member their names. But maybe
not. Whatever their names, wherever I see them, they're Ma's iris."*

Bill Nunn
"Ma's Iris"
Missouri Life
Volume 2, No. 2

The First One

Rising from last year's decay, the liverleaf blooms milky white, impatient with its own tardy leaves.

Daffodil Crock

Before the geraniums, before the petunias spill over its top, early morning's gold brightens the old earthenware.

Pink Buds

Encouraged by the first warm days, the flowering crab bursts into buds, eager to be the first to embrace Spring.

White Blossoms

And from the blue sky arching limitlessly beyond comes the tug of Somewhere, and it will not cease.

David's Car

But it's a long way back, to the house, when the car runs out of gas. But it will go again . . . soon.

Kite Wind

My heart
is with my kite,
Dipping,
Soaring,
Sailing,
out
of
sight.

Rebecca O'Hanlon Nunn

"Let's go fly a kite, up to the highest height,
Let's go fly a kite and send it soarrring . . ."

"Mary Poppins"
A Walt Disney Production
Words and music
by Richard M. and Robert S. Sherman
Buena Vista Records

Buffalo Clouds

In towering, galumphing shapes, they play hide-and-seek with the sun . . . and wind up our weather.

The Trio

And in trees still unleaved, the redbirds wait, unruffled, not yet stirred to this year's nesting.

Giant

*It's one hundred and six-
teen feet to the top of the
state champion sycamore
tree in Perry County . . .
but this one is still reaching.*

*Trees are short
and trees are tall,
and some grow leaves
to scuff in fall.*

*Trees are fat
and trees are thin
with windows where
the sun looks in.*

Aileen Fisher
Cricket in a Thicket
Charles Scribner's Sons, 1963

Taking Turns

Reaching for day's last sun, a day lily reigns over the rail fence . . . until the Double Dixie takes over.

The Floater

At blooming time, its trailing stems rise up and the toothed leaflets of the cinquefoil surround the "unbranched" one.

From the Window

Here she writes . . . and looks. And outside the rose blooms tall, and blooms again.

Acres of Susans

"I like how . . . when you mowed, how you left those . . ." Ted didn't call them weeds, and he didn't laugh. And the Black-eyed Susans bloomed all summer long.

Sarah

"Earth, tell any child that you are his forever, that he is the happy owner of a tilting world . . .

Tell him, Earth, that he has deed and title to beauty by the acre anywhere he breathes!"

Frances Frost
"Tell Any Child"
Life's Greatest Treasure
Hallmark Editions, 1968

"I Believe"

"The groves were God's first temples."

Arthur Cullen Bryant
"A Forest Hymn"

And in October the forest cathedral beckons whosoever will to its autumnal anthem.

Sassafras Silk

Overnight, ready to snare prey for him—and morning's early light for me—the spider has spun his skein in the back porch sassafras tree.

"What's miraculous about a spider's web?" said Mrs. Arable. "I don't see why you say a web is a miracle —it's just a web."

"Ever try to spin one?" asked Dr. Dorian."

E. B. White
Charlotte's Web
Harper & Row, 1952

Dogwood Design

*Another, with instinctive de-
sign, drapes the dogwood—
like the web, a deceptive
blend of beauty and
strength.*

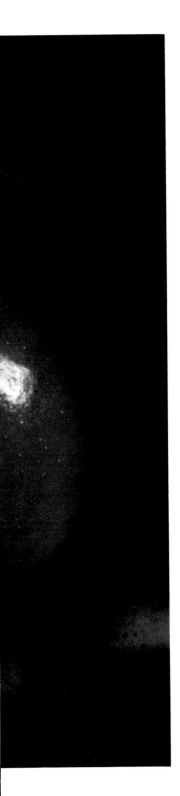

Bushel of Red

"... And when you can pass a winter's night by the fireside with no thought of the fruit at your elbow, then be assured you are no longer a boy, either in heart or years."

John Burroughs

Sunlit

"I have individual likings for many species that they (neighbors) lump under one aspersive category: brush."

Aldo Leopold
A Sand County Almanac
Oxford University Press, 1949

Windless

Cold, still, silent in the snow, the windmill seeks comfort and companionship with the silo.

Frost Finch

"They look like sparrows who, late on New Year's Eve, fell headlong into the wine."

Dion Henderson
A Season of Birds
Tamarack Press, 1976

Winter Tears

Big and moist, the snows of March melt quickly, and the oaks weep tears of gladness for the coming of Spring.

And Another Day . . .

"If you can fill the unforgiving minute
With sixty seconds' worth of distance run,
Yours is the Earth and everything that's in it,
And—which is more—You'll be a Man, my son!"

Rudyard Kipling
"If"

Missouri is . . .
The Bluebird

THEY came back early this year. He arrived first, watching warily from the old dead tree at woods' edge, then dipping in brilliant blue flashes to the box they shared last year, raising five healthy young ones.

The sparrows hadn't moved in yet, and he was delighted, eager to show her how neat the old place looked. She was

pleased, too, after a quick look around. Some new grass, and they'd be ready for housekeeping again.

Those other places they'd been, strange lands far beyond the hills and the crooked river, were all right for visiting . . . but not for real living and raising a family.

They talked happily, looking out over the familiar surroundings—the open field out front, with the power line at the far end for safe sitting; the fence row behind the house, a tangled thicket of trees and bushes; the woods, thick with blue-berried cedars . . .

It all looked the same, and together they agreed.

"It's good to be home again."

"To witness a bluebird courtship in early spring is well worth watching and waiting for. It contains all of the elements of tenderness, love, and devotion of the finest human relationship."

Lawrence Zeleny
The Bluebird
Indiana University Press, 1976

MISSOURI
BY BILL NUNN

was designed by Bill Nunn,
photocomposed in Goudy Old Style,
and printed on Warren's Flokote Enamel,
by The Lowell Press
115 East 31st Street, P.O. Box 1877, Kansas City, Missouri 64141

THE PONY EXPRESS
St. Joseph, Missouri

Sam Clemens of Hannibal
"Mark Twain"

Harry S. Truman

Helen Beck ~ "Sally Rand"

Kate Chopin ~ author of
"The Awakening"

Thomas Hart Benton

Scott Joplin

George Washington Carver

R. HAYNES